Science World

General editors · David & Simon Jolla

Keith Porter

Looking at Animals

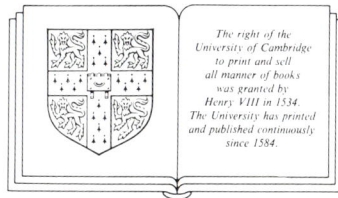

The right of the
University of Cambridge
to print and sell
all manner of books
was granted by
Henry VIII in 1534.
The University has printed
and published continuously
since 1584.

CAMBRIDGE UNIVERSITY PRESS

Cambridge · London · New York · New Rochelle · Melbourne · Sydney

Contents

What are animals?	5
From smallest to largest	6
Life on six legs	8
Butterflies and moths	10
The zoo in the home	12
On the seashore	14
Life in water	16
In and out of water	18
Reptiles	20
Feathers and wings	22
Birds which do not fly	24
Mammals	26
Animals with pouches	28
Mammals in the sea	30
Small gnawing animals	32
The cat family	34
Bears	36
Animals with hoofs	38
Apes and monkeys	40
The largest animals	42
Animals we must protect	44
Glossary	45
Index	47

Photographic credits

t = top   b = bottom   l = left   r = right   c = centre

5 Herwarth Voigtmann/Seaphot; 6/7 Stephen Dalton/NHPA; 7 Jonathan Scott/Seaphot; 8 Stephen Dalton/NHPA; 10 Hans Christian Heap/Seaphot; 11 Stephen Dalton/NHPA; 16 Herwarth Voigtmann/Seaphot; 17 Peter David/Seaphot; 22 A.P. Barnes/Seaphot; 23t Keith Scholey/Seaphot; 23b Stephen Dalton/NHPA; 25t ANT/NHPA; 25b Anthony Bannister/NHPA; 27t Jonathan Scott/Seaphot; 27b ANT/NHPA; 29 Oxford Scientific Films; 34 G. Lythgoe/Seaphot; 35 Sean T. Avery/Seaphot; 37t ZEFA; 37b S.J. Krasemann/NHPA; 38 John Lythgoe/Seaphot; 38/39 Peter Johnson/NHPA; 39 Jonathan Scott/Seaphot; 42 Ocean Images/Seaphot; 42/43 Sean T. Avery/Seaphot; 43 Steve Robinson/NHPA

Illustrations by David Anstey, Sallie Alane Reason

NOTE TO THE READER: while you are reading this book you will notice that certain words appear in **bold type**. This is to indicate a word listed in the Glossary on page 45. This glossary gives brief explanations of words which may be new to you.

Published by the
Press Syndicate of the University of Cambridge
The Pitt Building, Trumpington Street, Cambridge CB2 1RP
32 East 57th Street, New York, NY 10022, USA
10 Stamford Road, Oakleigh, Melbourne 3166, Australia

© BLA Publishing Limited 1987

First published 1987

British Library cataloguing in publication data

Porter, Keith
   Looking at animals. — (Science world).
   1. Animals — Juvenile literature
  I. Title   II. Series
  591   QL49

ISBN 0-521-33241-9

Designed and produced by BLA Publishing Limited, Swan Court, East Grinstead, Sussex, England.

A member of the **Ling Kee Group**
LONDON · HONG KONG · TAIPEI · SINGAPORE · NEW YORK

Colour origination by Waterden Reproductions Limited
Printed in Italy by New Interlitho

What are animals?

The world is full of living things. They are either plants or animals. Plants stay in one place and use sunshine to make their food. Animals cannot make their own food, so they have to search for it.

Animals differ in size and shape. Some are so tiny that we need a microscope to see them. Others, like the blue whale, are huge. There are many thousands of different kinds of animal.

Animals in groups

The study of animals tells us that they can be divided into a number of groups. All the birds belong to one group. There is another group for fish. Lizards, snakes, turtles, tortoises and crocodiles belong to a group called the **reptiles**. Frogs and toads belong to another group, called the **amphibians**. All the animals which give birth to live young, instead of laying eggs, are called **mammals**. Humans are mammals, so are dogs, cats and monkeys. The biggest group of animals is formed by the insects.

Animals must catch or find food to stay alive. They must be able to move to do this. Some simple types of water animal do stay fixed in one place. They feed on tiny bits of food which float in water. Most water animals have to swim about to find food. Land animals must walk, run, jump or fly. The animals that can move over the greatest distance are the birds.

▼ A large number of animals live under the water. In this picture of a coral reef you can see a shark and many smaller fish.

From smallest to largest

The body of an animal is made up of tiny parts called **cells**. Large animals are made of millions of cells. There are many types of simple animal which are too small to see. Some of these are made up of just one cell.

The simplest animals

The most simple animals live in water. They are so small that even one drop of pond water contains lots of them. These tiny animals belong to a group called the **protozoa**. This name means 'first animals'. Scientists think that the first living animals were like protozoa. The amoeba is one type of simple animal. It looks like a tiny blob of jelly. The amoeba's body is made from one cell. It moves by flowing along like a drop of water.

There are many other types of protozoa. Some move and feed by putting out parts of the cell like tiny 'feet'. Others are covered in tiny hairs. They wave these to move through the water.

Some protozoa can make copies of themselves by dividing in two. Then each half becomes a new animal.

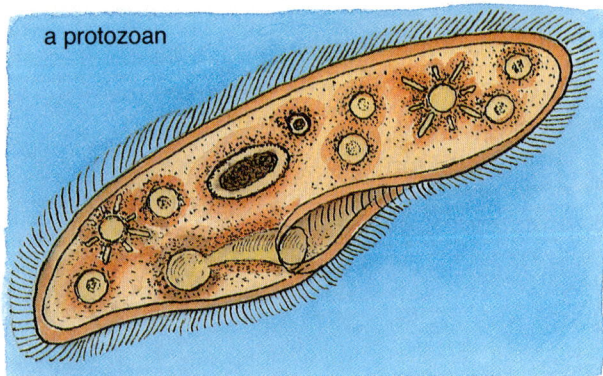

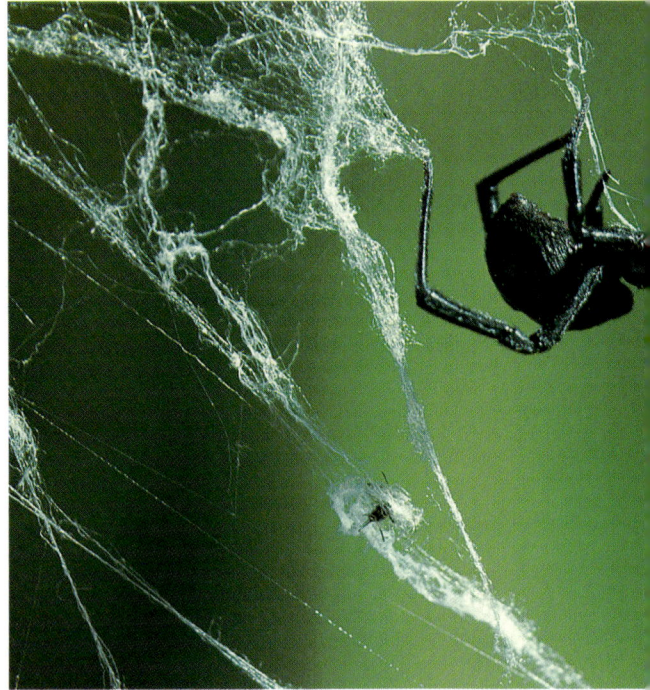

a protozoan

Animals without a backbone

Animals made up of many cells can be sorted into two types. We do this by looking at the way their bodies are built. Animals with bones and backbones are called **vertebrates**. Those without backbones are called **invertebrates**.

Most invertebrates are small. They include spiders, worms and insects. A tough outer skin gives shape to their bodies. The skin protects and supports the parts of the body.

The bumble bee bat, found in Thailand, is the lightest of all mammals. These tiny bats weigh between 1¾ and 2 grams.

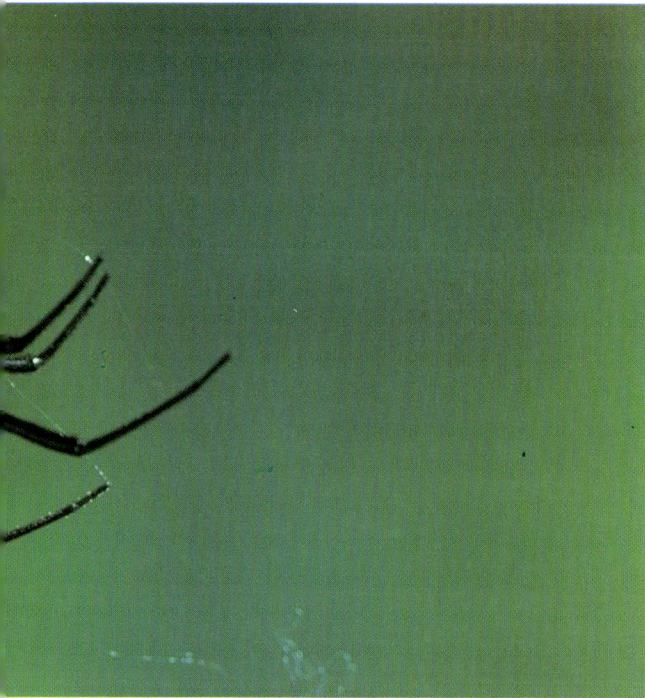

▲ Spiders are invertebrates. The Black Widow spider has a poisonous bite.

Animals with backbones

Other animals need more than their skin to support the weight of their bodies. They have hard bones beneath the skin. These bones all join up to form a **skeleton**. This gives the body its natural shape. The main part of the skeleton is the backbone. This helps to support the small bones and the soft parts of an animal's body.

Fish, amphibians, reptiles, birds and mammals all have backbones. Birds and bats have light skeletons so that they can fly in the air. Some tiny bats weigh less than two grams. Some elephants, on the other hand, weigh more than seven tonnes. Their leg bones have to be very thick and strong to carry this weight.

▼ The African elephant is the largest land animal. It is a vertebrate.

7

Life on six legs

Insects make up one of the largest groups of animals. There are over one million different types of insect. All of them have a hard skin and six legs. Many have two pairs of wings. Flies, beetles, bees and butterflies are all insects.

Insect bodies

The skin of an insect is hard and tough. It is made of a number of stiff sections. It is rather like a suit of armour. This hard, outside skeleton is called an **exoskeleton**. It gives shape to the insect and protects its body. It also stops its body from drying out.

All insects are made up of three main parts. One of these is the head. The head holds the eyes, mouth and feelers. The middle part is called the **thorax**. This is full of muscles. The wings and legs are fixed to the thorax and are moved by the muscles. The largest part of the body is called the **abdomen**. This contains the stomach and insides of the insect.

Thousands of types

Insects vary greatly in shape. Some, like stick insects, are long and thin. Others, like dung beetles, have large, rounded bodies. Most insects have wings and many of them are good fliers. Dragonflies can fly as fast as 25 kph, and some butterflies can fly a great distance across the sea.

Each type of insect is shaped to suit its own way of life. Insects that eat leaves have feet that can cling on to plants. Those that grab other insects and eat them have strong front legs and sharp jaws.

▼ There are more than 250 000 types of beetle. Stag beetles can be recognized by their large jaws.

▲ Locusts have three life stages. Butterflies have four life stages.

▼ An insect has three main parts to its body.

abdomen

thorax

head

Life in stages

The lives of insects are divided into a number of stages. Some insects have three stages, and others have four. Those with three, such as a locust, begin life as an egg. The egg hatches into a **nymph**, which looks like a small adult without wings. At the third stage the nymph becomes an adult.

Insects with four life stages, such as butterflies, go through much greater changes. The eggs hatch into **larvae** which do not look like their parents at all. A caterpillar, for example, is a larva of a butterfly. When the larva is fully grown it is ready for the next stage of its life.

This is called the **pupa** stage. A pupa cannot walk or eat. It is a 'shell' inside which an **adult** insect develops. When it is ready to do so, the adult insect breaks its way out of the pupa. The skin of the new adult is very soft. It soon dries out and becomes hard.

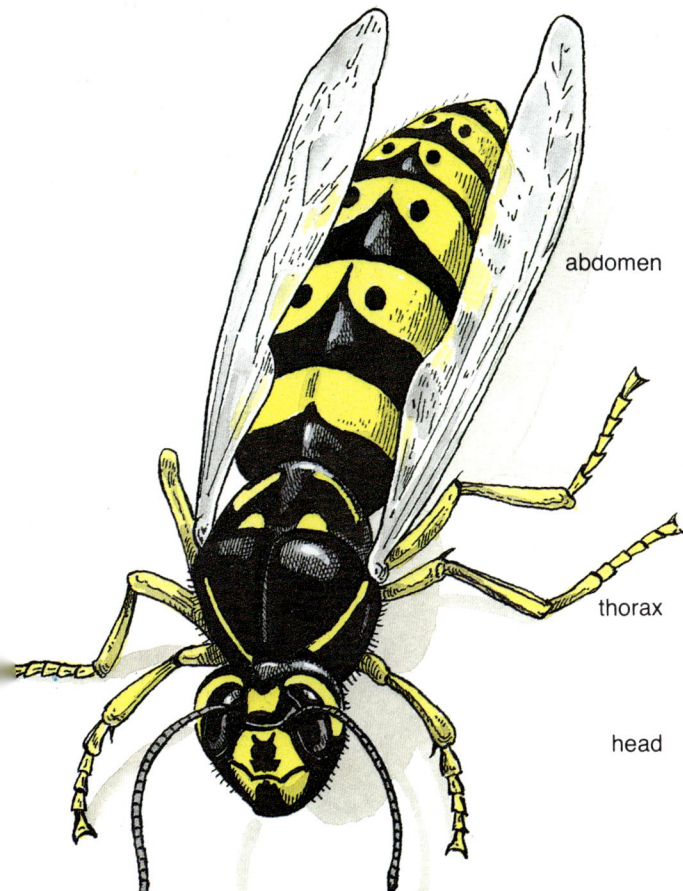

9

Butterflies and moths

There are more than 160 000 types of butterflies and moths. Do you know the difference between a butterfly and a moth? Most butterflies have brighter colours than moths. They fly in the daytime. Most moths fly at night and are dull in colour. Some moths come out in the daytime and may be as bright as butterflies. Many moths have furry bodies to keep them warm in the cold night air.

Butterflies and moths vary in size. The largest butterfly is found in Papua New Guinea. Its wings can be more than 28 cm across. The smallest of all is a moth, with wings only 2 mm across.

An amazing change

The larvae of moths and butterflies are caterpillars. They look like fat worms with tiny legs. Each one becomes a pupa when fully grown. Inside the pupa a new butterfly or moth takes shape.

When the adult breaks out of the pupa, its wings are at first crumpled. Soon the air dries the wings and they unfold. The crawling caterpillar has now become a butterfly. Few other animals go through such an amazing change.

▼ A caterpillar feeding on a flower. Most caterpillars feed on leaves or flowers.

Wings for flight

Butterflies and moths are good fliers. Most have a slow, flapping flight. Hawkmoths fly very fast. Their wings beat so fast that we can see only a blur when they fly.

The wings of these insects are very thin. Each side is covered in tiny flat **scales**, like the tiles on a roof. Each scale differs in colour to make up the wing pattern. Butterflies recognize each other by their wing patterns. Some have patterns that protect them. The bold 'eyes' on the wings of the peacock butterfly are there to scare off birds.

A few of these insects contain poisons. They warn their enemies by their bright markings. The orange and black of the monarch butterfly warns off birds. A few types are coloured to look like the monarch. They pretend to be poisonous, though they are not. These are called **mimics**. They use a kind of trickery to protect themselves.

Finding the way

Butterflies and moths are different in other ways. Butterflies have thin feelers, or **antennae**, with a knob at the tip. Moths can have feathery or thin antennae, without a knob.

These feelers are used like 'noses'. Butterflies trap scent and use it to recognize others of their kind. Most moths cannot see each other in the dark. The female moth gives out a special scent to attract males. The female emperor moth can attract a male from up to five kilometres away.

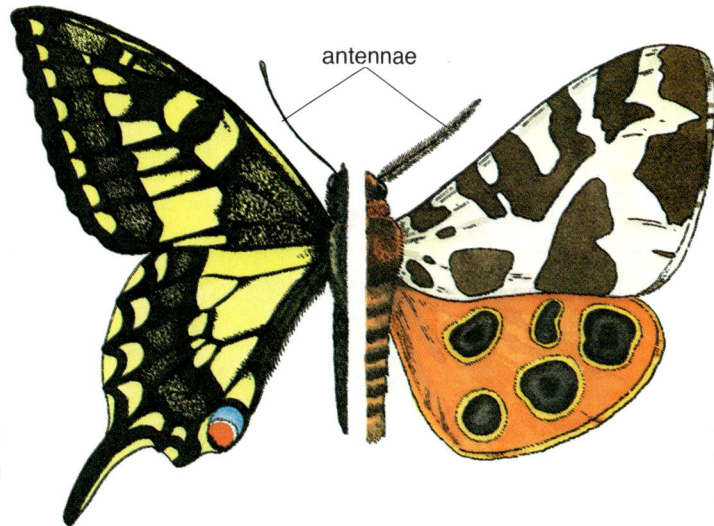

antennae

This drawing shows half a butterfly and half a moth. Look at the antennae. Can you spot which is the butterfly and which is the moth?

▼ A monarch butterfly.

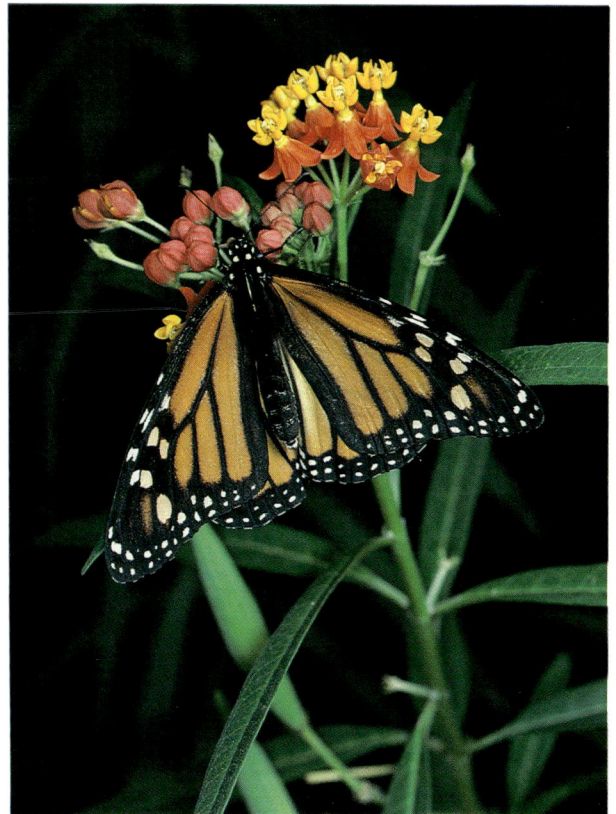

11

The zoo in the home

Many small animals live in your home. They include spiders, woodlice, centipedes and insects. Many of them hide during the daytime. Some live under cupboards and others crawl away into cracks. Most of these small animals do no harm. A few can spoil food or carry diseases.

Hidden from view

Some small animals live all the year round in houses. House crickets and cockroaches live in warm houses, feeding on crumbs and scraps of food. They hide in dark corners in the day. As night falls they creep out to feed. If a light is switched on, they hurry back to hide in the shadows.

Spiders like to live in dark corners. They spin their webs where the duster cannot reach. Most are harmless, but some, like the black widow spiders, are very poisonous. Black widows live in houses in some hot countries.

Some small animals will live only in damp parts of a house. The damp helps to stop their bodies from drying out. Woodlice need damp places to hide in. They come out at night to search for small scraps of food. Most gardens have woodlice in them. You will find them if you turn over stones or pieces of rotting wood. They often come indoors in the winter to find warmth and food.

What to look for

How do we know what animals live in our homes? Many of them appear only at night. First you need to know where to look.

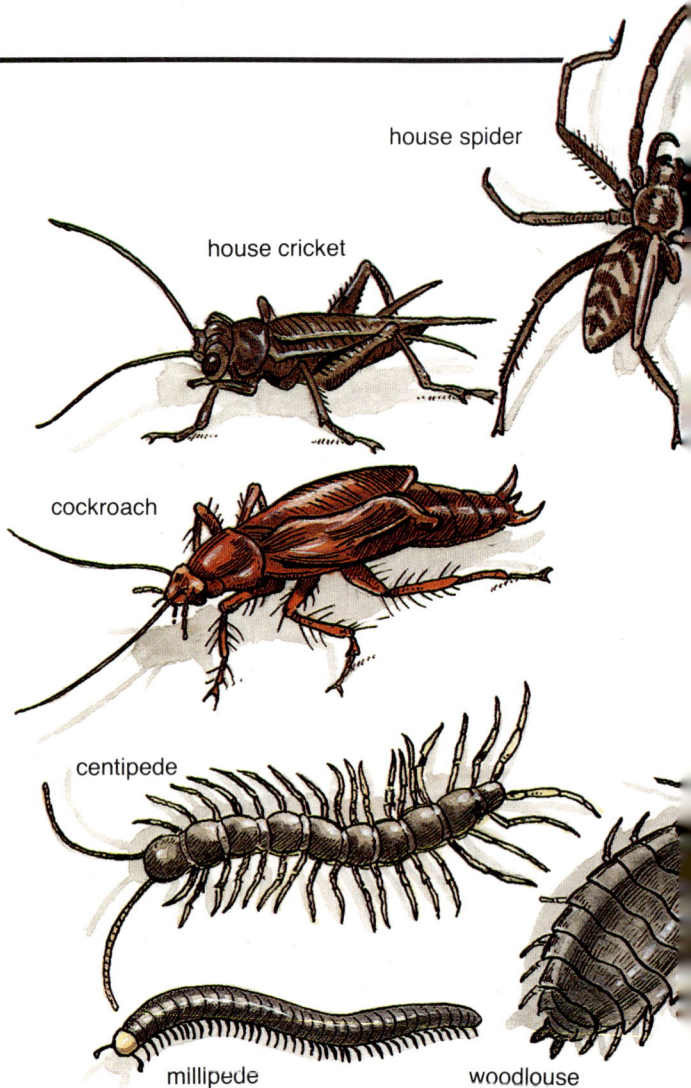

▲ Have you seen some of these animals around your house? You may need to look very closely in dark, damp corners, or at night.

Crickets and cockroaches like warm places. Good places to look are kitchens, and around fireplaces, hot pipes and boilers. Crickets are easy to find if you listen. Male crickets make a chirping sound. They do this to attract a female.

Woodlice, centipedes and millipedes all like damp places. Try looking in the

small tortoiseshell butterfly

ladybird

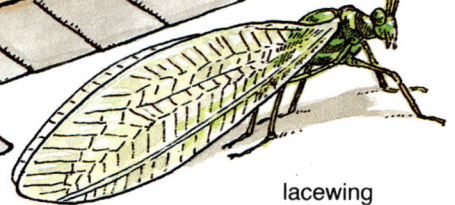

lacewing

bathroom or under the kitchen sink. Damp cellars are also good places to look.

Spiders can be found all over the home. Most spiders come out of hiding at night. You might see them if you shine a torch across a room in the dark.

Try to find out the names of the different animals you find. Keep a record of where they live. Remember that some of the small animals are useful. They catch and eat flies and other pests which harm us.

Shelter from the cold

Many small animals come into our homes for food and shelter. Ladybirds and lacewings come into homes to sleep, or **hibernate**, through the winter months. So do some butterflies. Houses give them better shelter than places in the open.

Some small animals come in for food. Fleas often feed on our cats and dogs. Fleas, mosquitoes and bed bugs come in to feed on us! This type of small animal is the greatest nuisance to us.

13

On the seashore

Twice each day, the sea moves slowly up and down the shore. These movements are called the **tides**. The highest point the sea reaches is called the high-tide mark. The lowest point is called the low-tide mark. The sea covers the lower part of the beach for most of the day.

Types of beach

Perhaps you have been to the sea at different places. Some beaches are rocky with lots of pebbles. Others are sandy and flat. Each type is home for different animals. Some animals prefer to live on the rocks. Others burrow in the sand.

Many animals which live on the seashore can live in and out of water. Some are better at doing this than others. Barnacles can live on rocks high up the beach. They can keep tightly closed when the tide is out. Crabs need to keep fairly damp, so they live in the lower part of the beach.

Rock pools

Rock pools are small pools of sea water. The water stays in the pools when the tide goes out. Often you can see shrimps, crabs and small fish. Most of the time they hide under the stones in the pools. Sea anemones, limpets and mussels cling to rocks around the pool. They live there all the time. Larger fish are sometimes left behind when the sea goes out.

Under the sand

At first, you only see empty sea shells on a sandy beach. These once contained living animals. Many of these animals burrow beneath the sand. Razor shells and cockles have a strong 'foot' to pull their shells under the sand.

Other signs of life are small pits or tubes in the sand. These are made by sea worms. Thousands of types of sea worm live in the sea. Some burrow under the sand. Others build tubes which poke out of the sand.

As the tide comes in, it brings the sand to life. Starfish, crabs and sea

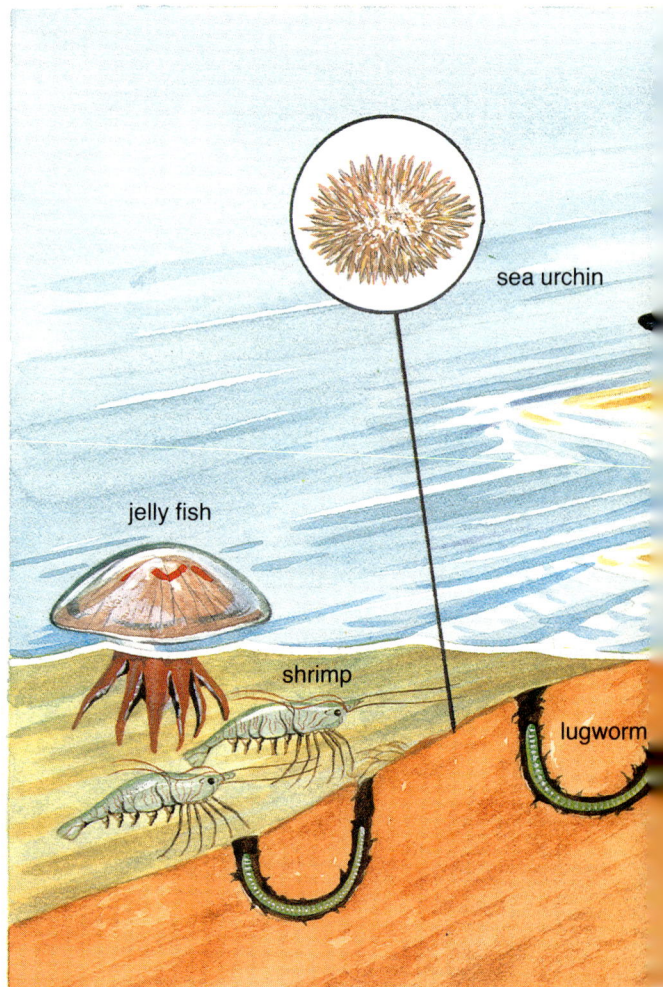

sea urchin

jelly fish

shrimp

lugworm

urchins dig their way to the surface. Small holes appear in the sand where the worms push through. Shoals of small fish return with the tide.

Most of the seashore animals feed on tiny pieces of food. Some use fine 'nets' of waving hairs to trap food from the water. Others use sticky threads to trap food. Sea anemones and crabs eat other animals. All the seashore animals have different ways of keeping alive.

▼ A razor shell burrows by pushing its foot into the sand. Then the tip of the foot swells and pulls down the shell.

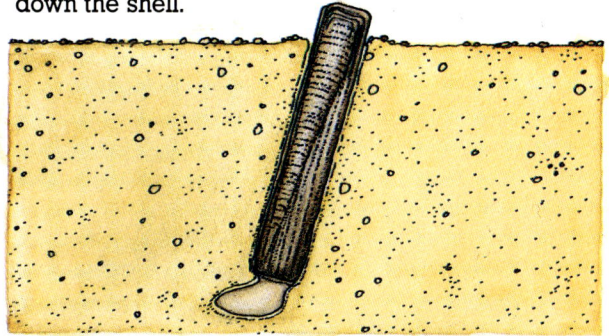

oyster catcher

cockle

mussel

limpet

starfish

sea anemone

shore crab

barnacle

Life in water

It is easy to think that the seas and oceans are just large masses of water which divide the Earth's land. In fact, there is more life in the water than there is on land.

Life began in water millions of years ago. This was a long time before life reached the land.

Most of the world's water is sea water, which contains salt. Some water animals cannot live in salty water. They live in the fresh water of the rivers, ponds and lakes.

How fish breathe

All animals need to breathe. This is because they need a gas called oxygen. Oxygen helps them to get energy from their food. Land animals get oxygen from the air. Fish get oxygen from the water.

Fish have a different way of breathing from us. They swim along opening and closing their mouths. Water passes down the throat and then out through holes on the side of the head. These holes contain thin pieces of skin called **gills**, which are full of tiny blood vessels. The water passing over the gills contains oxygen. This gas moves out of the water and through the gills into the blood. The fish's heart pumps the blood all around the body. This is how oxygen reaches all parts of the fish.

Food for all

All water animals need food. Many of them feed on water plants. Plants need sunlight to grow, so they must live near the surface. Sunlight reaches only about 50 m below the surface.

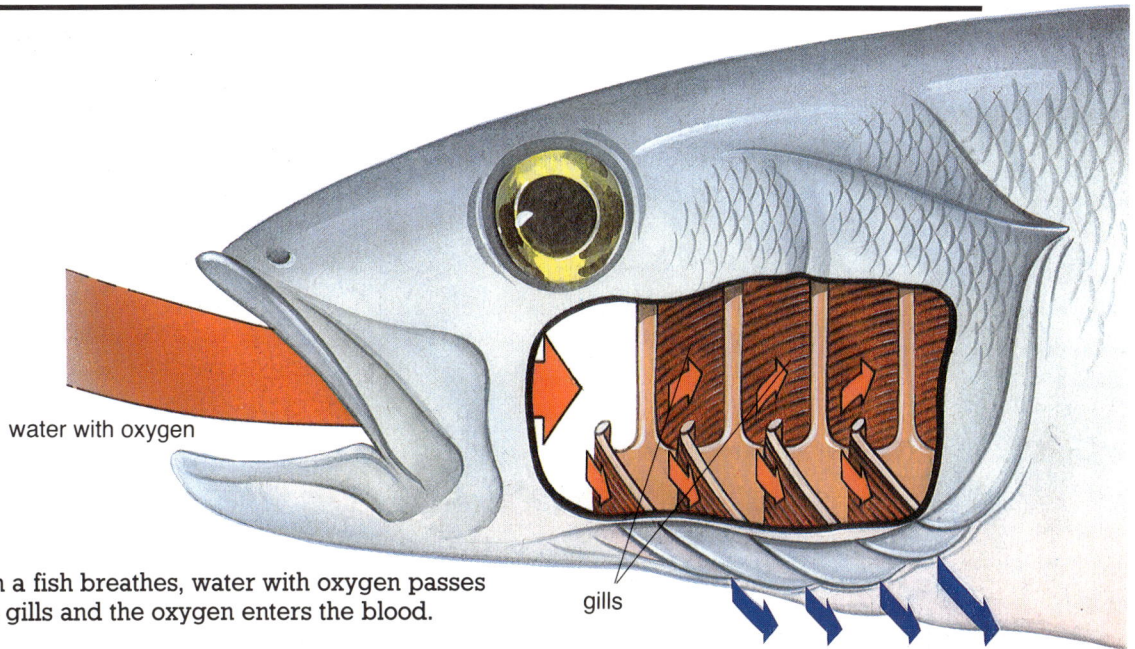

▶ When a fish breathes, water with oxygen passes over the gills and the oxygen enters the blood.

water with oxygen

gills

Tiny plants and animals called **plankton** float near the surface. They are so small that they look like tiny specks. Many larger animals feed on the plankton. They include the young of fish, crabs and other animals. These are eaten in turn by adult fish, jellyfish and other sea animals.

Animals which feed on others are called **predators**. Sharks are some of the most deadly predators. They can catch almost anything they want to.

Life in the deep

The deepest oceans reach thousands of metres in depth. It is dark and cold deep down. The animals that live in these dark depths are in another world. They never come to the surface. Many feed on the remains of dead animals that sink down from the surface. Others are predators. They hunt each other in the dark.

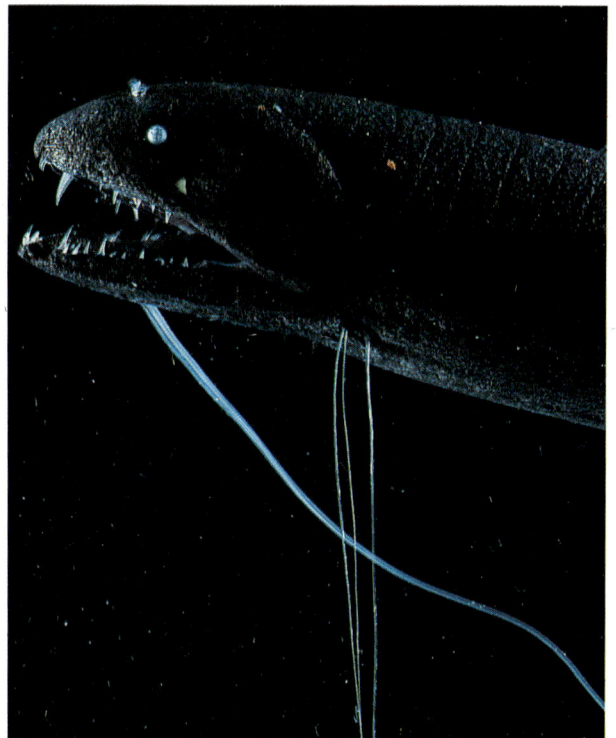

▲ A deep sea fish. Most deep sea fish never come to the surface.

In and out of water

Some different kinds of amphibian.

natterjack toad

tropical tree frog

smooth newt

long-tailed salamander

One group of animals, the amphibians, can live in and out of water. They include frogs and toads. All amphibians begin life in water. A fully grown amphibian can live away from water, but most keep close to wet places. Their skin must not get too dry.

The life of the frog

Frogs breed in the spring. They collect together in large numbers near water. The female frogs become very fat. Their bodies are full of eggs, or **spawn**. These eggs are laid in shallow water. Unlike birds' eggs, they have no shell. The black egg is protected by a clear jelly. The jelly is full of food for the growing frog.

The young frog is called a **tadpole**. Tadpoles grow very quickly. They begin as a dark blob with a tail. After a week or so the tadpole wriggles free of the jelly. It has no front or back legs. Tadpoles eat tiny water plants and animals. Some even eat smaller tadpoles. Soon, they grow legs, the back legs appearing first, then the front legs. At the same time, the tail shrinks. The tadpole begins to look like a tiny frog.

How amphibians breathe

Tadpoles have feathery gills. These help them to get oxygen from the water. Like fish, tadpoles cannot live out of water. As their legs grow, the gills disappear.

The tiny frog can breathe in other ways. It can use its thin skin like a gill. Oxygen from water passes through the skin. It enters the tiny blood vessels beneath the skin. This kind of breathing can happen only if the skin is wet. The adult frogs are able to breathe air to get oxygen. They have **lungs**, just like birds, reptiles and mammals do. This means that adult frogs can live away from water.

Many types

Amphibians include frogs, toads, newts and salamanders. There are over 4000 different types. Most frogs and toads live on the ground but a few types live in trees. The fingers of these frogs have suckers. These help them to cling to smooth leaves.

Salamanders and newts look a bit like lizards. They have long tails and four short legs. Unlike lizards, their skin is smooth and never scaly. The largest amphibian is a salamander. One type in China can grow to 180 cm in length. This giant amphibian spends most of its life in water.

The life cycle of a frog.

adult frog

young frog loses tail

tadpole grows legs and lungs

frogspawn

tadpole with hindlegs

tadpole with gills

19

Reptiles

A reptile's body

Turtles have flippers for swimming in water. Apart from snakes, which have no legs, all other reptiles have short legs. Their skin is covered in tough scales. These scales protect the body and make it waterproof. Some reptiles, like turtles and crocodiles, spend most of their lives in water.

Dinosaurs and other animals ruled the Earth 200 million years ago. These animals belonged to the group we call the reptiles. The reptiles of today include lizards, snakes, tortoises, turtles and crocodiles.

We can recognize reptiles by their shape and skin. Lizards have long scaly bodies and a tail. Their legs spread out sideways. Crocodiles look like large lizards. Their scales are thick and leathery. They have very sharp teeth. Snakes are rather like lizards without legs. They wriggle along on their bellies.

Turtles are shaped for life in the water. Their legs and feet have become strong flippers. They can use them for swimming or for moving on land. The scales on their shells are smooth so that they can move through water easily.

Some different kinds of reptiles.

alligator

rattlesnake

green lizard

tortoise

terrapin

Giant reptiles called dinosaurs lived millions of years ago.

Reptiles and their young

Reptiles produce young by laying eggs. In some types of reptile the eggshells are leathery, in others they are hard. The young reptiles feed on a liquid inside the shell. Soon they grow strong enough to break out of the shell. They hatch out as small copies of their parents.

Reptiles of the past

The world was once full of giant reptiles. The dinosaurs died out millions of years ago. They became **extinct**. We know that they lived because their remains have been found in rocks. These remains are called **fossils**.

The best known reptiles were the dinosaurs. The giant Brachiosaurus was the largest of these. It was 12 m tall and 23 m long. Most of these giants ate plants. Their teeth were shaped like pegs.

A few, like the Tyrannosaurus, had huge, sharp teeth. They chased and ate other dinosaurs. The scales of some dinosaurs were thick and strong. They needed this armour to protect them from their enemies. There were also reptiles that could swim and some had wings for flying.

Reptiles today

The reptiles of today are not so large as those of long ago. But many of them are just as fierce. Crocodiles and alligators all live by eating other animals.

There are almost 6000 types of snake and lizard. Most of these eat other animals. Some use poison, or **venom**, to kill their food. Most turtles are plant eaters. They have hard, horny jaws for biting.

Reptiles are **cold-blooded** animals. They cannot make their own body heat. This is why most of them live in warm countries.

Feathers and wings

The first birds flew millions of years ago. Scientists believe that the first birds developed, or **evolved**, from a group of reptiles. Their bodies changed over a very long time. Their scales became feathers. Their front legs became wings. They developed keen eyesight. These and other changes made it possible for them to fly and find their food.

Eggs and nests

All birds lay eggs with hard shells. The shell lets in air so the chick can breathe. A bird's egg contains lots of food. This is used by the growing chick.

Birds can be divided into two main groups. One group builds nests which hold the eggs and young. The parents have to bring food to the young in the nest. The young birds are called **nestlings**. They are blind and helpless when they hatch. The second group of birds use their nests for the eggs only. The chicks can run about as soon as they have hatched. They follow their parents and feed themselves. Ducks and chickens have this type of young.

▼ A family of bearded tits cry out for food. Parent birds feed their young for about 10 days by giving them half-eaten food.

Birds are **warm-blooded** animals. A warm-blooded animal can keep its body at a steady temperature. It makes its own body heat. It can also lose heat if it gets too hot.

Feathers and wings

The feathers of a bird help to keep it warm. This means that birds can feed and fly in cold places. Feathers also keep out water, which is very important for seabirds and wading birds. The wing feathers are important for flying.

A bird flies by flapping its wings. To do this, a bird needs a large heart and strong chest muscles. The wings push against the air. This lifts the bird off the ground. Once in the air, the shape of the bird's wings helps it to glide through the air. Some birds fly by **soaring**. They use the warm air which rises from the land. The rising air lifts them up into the sky.

▼ This picture shows how an owl's wings change shape during flight.

▲ A condor soars above the cliffs in Peru. It is making use of the rising air currents.

Soaring birds, like the eagle, can stay in the air for a long time without flapping their wings.

The smallest bird is the bee humming bird. It is only six centimetres long and weighs under two grams. One of the largest birds is the albatross. It has a wingspan of about 3.5 m. There are nearly 9000 types of bird in the world.

Birds which do not fly

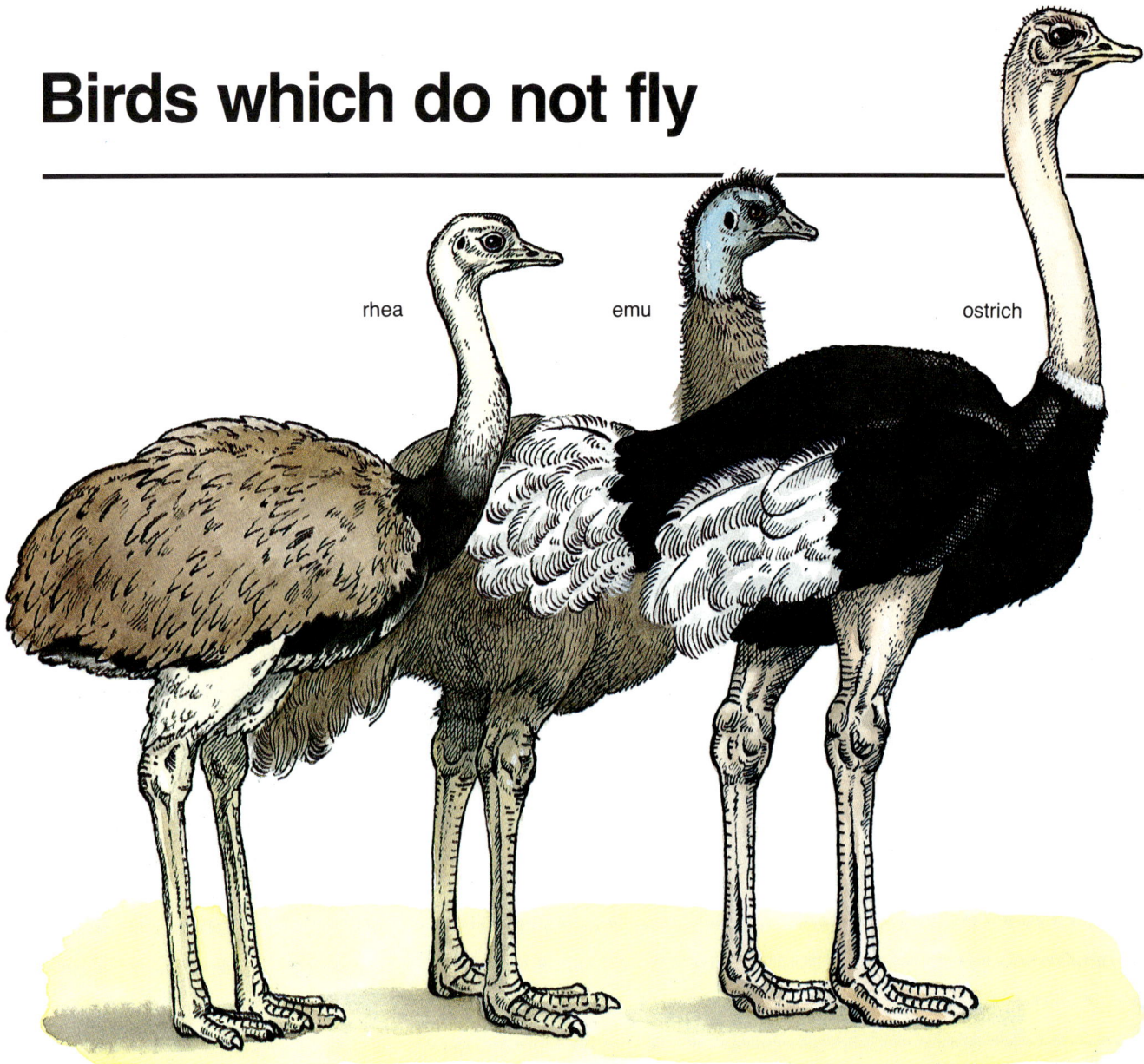

rhea

emu

ostrich

The largest birds

The ostrich, emu and rhea are large running birds with strong legs. The ostrich is the heaviest living bird, weighing up to 135 kg and reaching 2.5 m in height. The ostrich can run at speeds up to 60 kph, which helps it to run from danger. Ostriches live in open grassland, where there are many predators. If attacked, they kick out with their strong feet. These birds often live together in herds for safety.

The rhea, emu and ostrich are too big and heavy to fly.

A few types of bird cannot fly. Their short wings are useless for flight. Some, like penguins, use their wings to swim. Others, like the ostrich, have long legs. They can run very fast.

Ostriches and rheas make large nests. Several females lay their eggs in one nest. A large number of eggs may be laid in a single nest. The male birds often watch over the nest and eggs. Emus do not share nests in this way.

▲ The kakapo from New Zealand is the biggest parrot in the world. It attempts to glide but cannot fly properly.

Penguins

Penguins are flightless seabirds. They live in the cold southern oceans. A penguin's wings are like stiff flippers. They are expert swimmers and can dive deep in their search for fish.

Like all seabirds, penguins make their nests on land. They are some of the few animals that can survive the bitter cold of Antarctica. A penguin has three 'overcoats'. The first is a tough outside layer of feathers. These are oily and keep water out. Beneath them is a layer of fluffy feathers called **down**. Down feathers are very good at keeping the cold out and warmth in. Finally, under the skin is a layer of fat, which is also good at keeping heat in.

Island birds

Some groups of flightless birds live on islands. The most famous of these is the kiwi. There are two types of kiwi and both live in New Zealand. They only come out to feed at night. Kiwis are now rare, because they are easy prey for hunting animals. They are now protected by law.

Other flightless birds were not so lucky. A bird called the dodo once lived on the island of Mauritius in the Indian Ocean. Dodos had no natural enemies until humans arrived. The dodos were easy to catch. Some were eaten by hungry sailors. Others were killed by the animals which people brought to the island. By 1746 all the dodos had been killed.

Several other island birds cannot fly and many others are poor fliers. The kakapo is a type of parrot which lives in the forests of New Zealand. It cannot fly, but climbs trees and glides to the ground.

▼ Penguins spend most of their lives at sea. There are 18 different types, including the Jackass penguins seen here.

Mammals

When you go to a zoo, you see many different animals. Most zoos have lions, elephants, bears, monkeys and seals. In your home, you may keep a pet dog or hamsters. These animals all seem very different, yet they all belong to one group. We call this group the mammals. There are many other types of animal in this group, including humans.

All mammals have backbones and they are warm-blooded. They have another thing in common. They give birth to live young. Very soon after they are born, young mammals start feeding on their mother's milk.

There are two unusual types of mammal that lay eggs. These are the duck-billed platypus and the spiny anteater. We still call these mammals because they feed milk to their young.

Animals with fur

Almost all mammals have fur to keep them warm. A few, such as ourselves, have lost the fur. We have a layer of fat beneath our skin. This helps to keep out the cold. We also wear clothes to keep warm.

Some mammals, such as whales and dolphins, live in the sea. They do not have fur. This would slow down their movement in water. Instead, they have a thick layer of fat, or **blubber**, under their skin. This keeps them warm in the cold seas. The blue whale is the largest of all animals. It is over 33 m long.

▼ The blue whale is the biggest animal that has ever lived.

▲ The topi is a kind of antelope which is found in Africa. Topis help each other by living in a herd.

How mammals behave

You can train a dog to obey simple commands. Some people have trained dolphins, elephants and other mammals. You could not do this with a fish, an insect or a reptile. They have smaller brains.

It is the size of their brains that has helped mammals to find their food and avoid their enemies. Mammals often live and work together to help each other. Animals, such as wolves, roam in packs. Each pack has a leader. The leader keeps the pack in order, and leads the pack when hunting for food.

Mammals that fly

As well as the many mammals that live on land or in the sea, there are the bats. This group of mammals contains about 800 types.

Bats are the only flying mammals. They fly mainly at night, when they search for insects and other food.

All kinds of mammal

There are about 4000 types of mammal. This is a small number compared with the one million types of insect. Mammals vary so much in size and shape that they are sorted into smaller groups or families.

The human is the most successful animal. It has the largest brain of all.

▼ The wings of a bat are made of very thin skin and bones. This is a ghost bat, from Australia. Can you guess how it gets its name?

Animals with pouches

The kangaroo is well known for its unusual shape. You may also know that young kangaroos begin life in a pouch below the mother's stomach. Kangaroos belong to a group of over 250 animals which all have pouches. They are called **marsupials**, or pouched mammals.

Inside the pouch

Marsupials are very small when they are born. A young kangaroo weighs just a few grams at birth. It has no fur and cannot see. The tiny baby crawls into the pouch. Inside the pouch are several **teats**, or nipples. The baby clings on to one of these and feeds on the milk. Some baby marsupials stay fixed to the teat for two months. Then they are large enough to leave the pouch. Some still return to the pouch for milk.

Bandicoots, wombats and the marsupial moles dig in the ground. Their pouches open to the rear. This is to stop them from filling with soil.

koala

cuscus

kangaroo

Some marsupials fro
Australia. In real life
the kangaroo is muc
bigger than the koal

Marsupials past

At one time there were many types of marsupial in the world. Most of them became extinct as they could not compete with other animal groups. Today, most marsupials are found in Australia. No other types of mammal reached Australia until people first went there. They introduced many animals, some of which were a danger to the marsupials.

Marsupials present

Some marsupials have survived elsewhere. They include the opossums, which are found in America. These small animals look like mice.

There are marsupials which look or behave like bears, monkeys, cats, rats, mice and wolves. This does not mean that they are related to each other. A koala 'bear' is not a bear at all. It behaves more like a monkey, since it lives in the trees. The cuscus and the bush-tailed possum are also like monkeys, with their long tails.

The Tasmanian devil

Meat-eating marsupials include animals which are like small cats and wolves. One of these, the Tasmanian devil, is about 90 cm long and has a black coat. It hunts small animals like frogs and mice, but it can also kill animals much larger than itself.

Long ago, there were marsupial tigers and lions. They died out, like many other marsupials. The Tasmanian wolf has not been seen since 1936. No one knows whether it is now extinct or not.

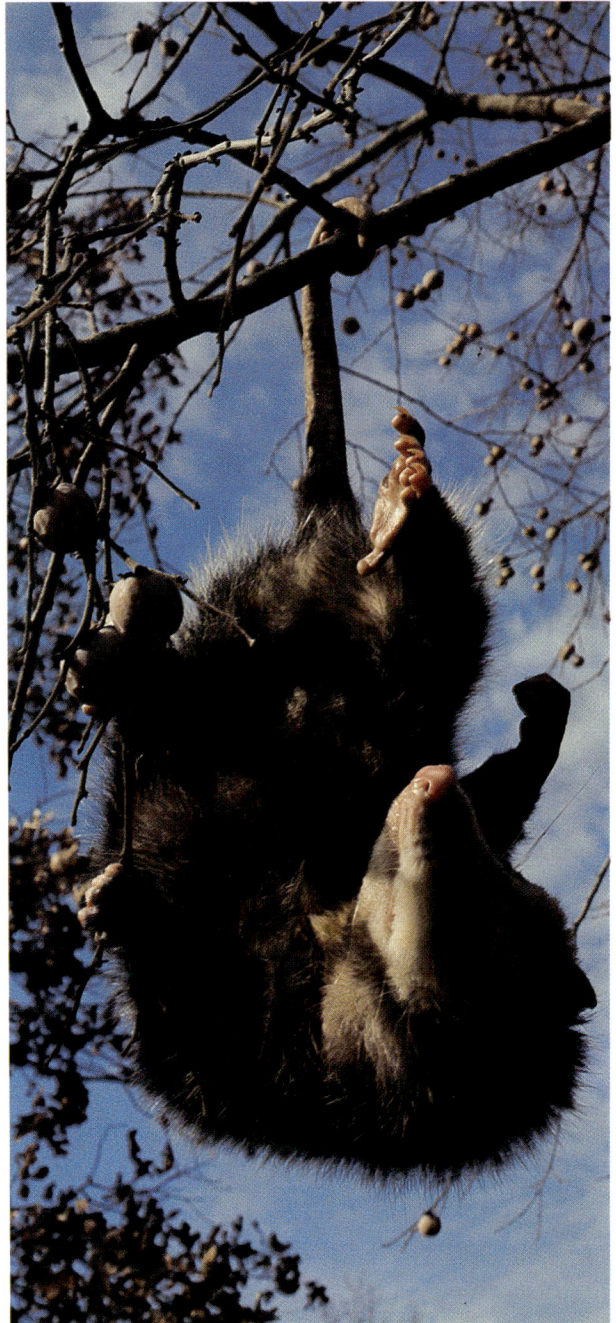

▲ This North American opossum looks fit and well. Sometimes opossums escape enemies by pretending to be dead. Have you heard the phrase 'playing 'possum'?

Mammals in the sea

killer whale

common dolphin

humpback whale

bottlenose dolphin

Some whales, dolphins, seals and walruses.

Some mammals live in the sea. Whales and dolphins look like large fish, but they are not fish. Their shape helps these mammals to swim through the water. They use their front flippers as 'arms' for steering. They swim through the water by waving their very powerful tails up and down.

Seals and walruses are also mammals. They have heads that look like those of dogs.

Whales and dolphins

There are 76 different types of whale and dolphin. Like all mammals, they give birth to live young. The young feed on their mother's milk under the water.

Whales and dolphins differ from fish in another way. Fish breathe using gills. Whales and dolphins use lungs to breathe air. They must come to the surface from time to time to take in air. The sperm whale can hold its breath for more than one hour. Other whales need to come to the surface more often.

A whale has a hole on the top of its head for breathing. It is called a **blowhole** and connects to the whale's lungs. When a whale comes to the surface to breathe it has to clear the blowhole. This can shoot a tall spout of water into the air.

The largest whales eat tiny sea animals. They strain these from the water through a kind of skin called **baleen**. The blue whale and the humpback whale feed like this. Other whales use teeth to eat fish. Dolphins and porpoises mainly eat small fish.

harp seal

walrus

Clever mammals

Dolphins are clever animals. They have quite large brains and can be taught to do tricks. Like whales, they make sounds which may be a way of 'talking' to each other. The songs of the humpbacked whales can be heard many kilometres away. They are known to make about 20 different sounds. These may make up a whale language. Perhaps one day we will be able to work it out.

Seals and walruses

Seals and walruses are also mammals. They have heads that look like dogs. Their flippers look more like feet. They need to use them when they come on to the land. Unlike whales, seals breathe through their mouths and nostrils.

Seals look clumsy on the land. Their bodies look fat and heavy. When they swim in the sea they look graceful. Their sleek bodies help them to swim quickly.

Most seals catch and eat fish. Walruses have tusks that are just large teeth. They dig shellfish out of the mud using their snouts and tusks. They also use their tusks as weapons when they fight each other.

The blue whale is the largest animal in the world. In 1947 a blue whale was caught by Russian fishermen. It weighed 190 tonnes. This is about half the weight of a fully laden Boeing 747 jumbo jet.

Small gnawing animals

More than a third of all animals belong to a group called the **rodents**. Most rodents, like mice, rats and squirrels, are small animals with big front teeth. There are a few larger rodents. The biggest, the capybara, is the size of a sheep.

Teeth for cutting

The name rodent comes from a word meaning 'to gnaw'. This tells us how these animals feed. They have four large front teeth. Two are fixed to the upper jaw and two to the bottom jaw. The teeth are very sharp and can cut through the hardest materials. Some rats have been known to chew through metal!

Many rodents eat plants and seeds. Some of these are pests. They eat the plants and seeds which humans grow for food. Rats can destroy stores of grain. Cane rats in West Africa eat huge amounts of sugar cane crops. Rats are sometimes pests in another way. They can carry diseases which kill people.

Rodents can breed very quickly. The lemming is one of the fastest breeders. A female lemming can produce six young every three to four weeks! Each young lemming can then produce its own young when it is only four weeks old. Huge numbers of these animals can build up very quickly.

Burrows, dens and dams

Most rodents like to feed at night, when their enemies cannot see them. During the day they sleep in burrows or nests. Some live alone. Others live in **colonies**. Prairie dogs live in burrows. They can

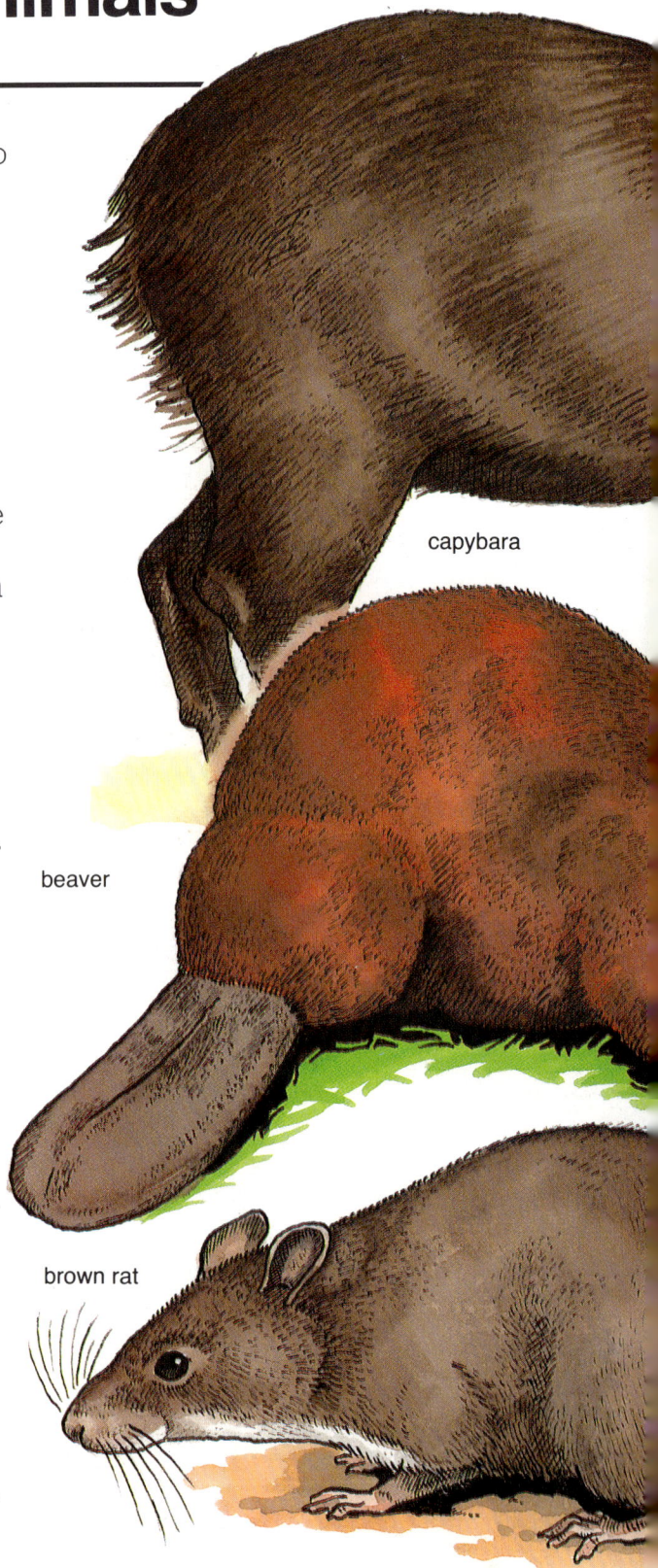

capybara

beaver

brown rat

prairie dog

take over huge areas of land. Some prairie dog 'towns' contain up to 5000 of these rodents.

The prairie dog is closely related to the squirrel. Some types of squirrel are called ground squirrels. They live in rocky dens or underground. Most squirrels live in the trees. They build their nests above ground in hollow tree trunks and branches.

Beavers are large rodents. They are well known for their building skills. They build large nests called **lodges** out of sticks and mud. First, a lodge is built. When the lodge is finished the beavers build a dam downstream. This makes a lake around the lodge, which protects the home from enemies.

Rabbits and hares

Rabbits and hares look like rodents. However, they differ in a number of ways. Because of these differences, rabbits and hares are placed in their own group. There are about 60 types of rabbit and hare around the world.

red squirrel

Some different kinds of rodents

deer mouse

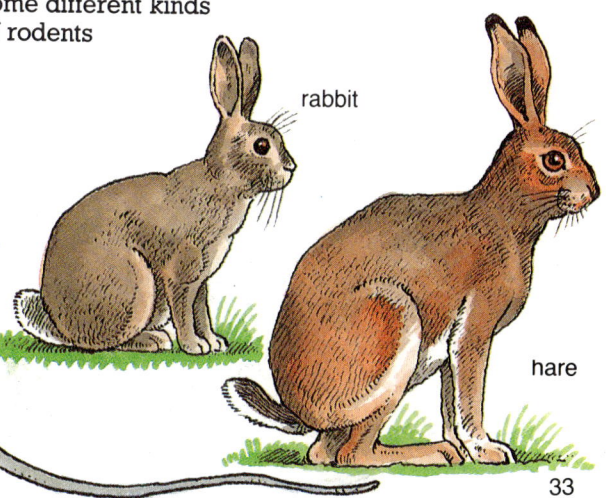
rabbit

hare

The cat family

It is very easy to recognize members of the cat family. They have certain things in common with the tame, or **domestic** cats which some people keep in their homes. If you have a pet cat you will know one thing for certain. It has very sharp teeth and claws.

If you watch a tame cat moving, you will soon learn why all cats are good at hunting. Cats can keep very still. They can creep forward very slowly, very near to the ground. Sometimes you will see them pouncing on a leaf, or even on a mouse. They can also run very fast.

Most cats can climb trees. When they fall, they always fall on their feet. They can twist their bodies easily as they fall through the air.

▲ This African lion is showing its big teeth, used for eating meat. Can you tell if it is a male or female lion?

Three different types of cat.

puma

serval

northern lynx

34

Cats in the wild

Most of the different types of small cat live in forests. Their coats have patterns of spots or stripes. These help them to hide in bushes or trees. They hunt small animals and creep up on them silently. Then they pounce to kill their food.

Many of the small cats hunt at night. In the dark, a cat can see six times better than we can. There are 28 types of small cat. The puma is the largest of these. It lives in North and South America.

The big cats

There are only seven different types of big cat. They are much larger than the small cats. All these big cats roar but they cannot purr like other cats. This is because of the way their throats are shaped.

Tigers and other forest cats stalk their prey. Cheetahs live in open country. They cannot creep up close to their prey without being seen. Instead, they can run faster than any other animal for a short distance. Then they can reach speeds of nearly 100 kph.

Lions live in groups called **prides**, but most other big cats live and hunt alone. Each animal protects its own hunting ground or **territory**. The big cats have nothing to fear from other animals. They rule the territory in which they hunt.

Lions often hunt together. They surround their prey before attacking. Male lions have long hair on their necks. This is called a **mane**. It makes the lion look larger. Males often fight each other for leadership of a pride. The largest, strongest male becomes the leader.

▼ Cheetahs have very keen eyes. They keep watch for prey such as jackals and hares.

Bears

Malayan sun bear

Asian black bear

sloth bear

▲ Three of the four types of small bear. The sloth bear is the largest and can grow to the size of a small pony.

Many people think of bears as lovable animals. In fact, although they may look friendly, they can be very fierce. They include the largest meat-eating land animals, the grizzly and polar bears.

In all, there are seven different types of bear. They all have thick fur, a short tail and small ears and eyes. Their large noses tell us that they have a good sense of smell.

Small bears

There are four types of small bear. All live in the forests of hot countries and all climb trees. They like to eat fruit, leaves and young roots. They also eat insects, small mammals and birds' eggs.

The sun bear and the South American spectacled bear are active all year. The sloth bear and the Asian black bear sleep for some of the year. They hide away in shelters or caves called dens. The young are born in the den.

The largest of these bears is the sloth bear. It looks like a shaggy dog, but is the size of a small pony. The sun bear is the smallest. It is the size of a large dog.

The grizzly bear

The grizzly, also called the brown bear, is a giant animal. Large males can weigh over 500 kg. Some grizzlies reach up to three metres tall when they are standing.

The grizzly is very fierce. It attacks anything which threatens its cubs. The only animal it needs to fear is the human. The grizzly once lived over a much wider area. Many thousands have been shot over the last 200 years. It used to live all over Europe, but today it is found only in parts of North America and Russia.

The grizzly has a large appetite. It mainly eats plant food, like leaves and berries. One of its favourite meals is salmon, which it catches in mountain streams. Grizzlies also catch larger animals, like deer.

▼ Grizzly bears feed on different kinds of food. They are expert at catching fish.

▲ Polar bears may look slow. In fact, they are good swimmers and can run very fast.

The grizzly spends the winter in a den. It lives off the body fat which it has stored up over the summer. The mother gives birth to young during the winter. The young are helpless at birth and stay in the den until the spring. They stay with their mother until they are between two and four years old.

The polar bear

The polar bear is a huge bear. Some males weigh over 700 kg. This white giant lives in the icy cold of the Arctic. Most of its life is spent on the ice and snow. It has a thick layer of fat beneath its coat to help keep the cold out.

The polar bear has long claws to help catch its food. The bear's favourite food is seal meat. The bear waits by holes in the ice for seals to come up for air. If a seal appears, it has little chance.

Animals with hoofs

Some mammals have claws on their feet. They use these for holding their prey or for climbing trees. The cats have to draw in their claws when they run after their prey.

Many large animals eat only plants and live in grassy places. They need to run to escape the predators. These animals have hoofs on their feet instead of claws.

Hoofs and horn

Hoofs are a kind of claw. Animals with hoofs are really walking on tiptoe. The hoof is made of the same material as finger nails. Like nails and claws, hoofs go on growing. The tip of the hoof is worn away as the animal walks or runs.

Many hoofed animals have horns. These have a hard bony centre. The outside of a horn is covered in the same material as hoofs. The **antlers** of a deer are not real horns. They are made of bone and have a velvet covering. The horns of a rhinoceros are made of hair. Layers of tough hair make up the solid rhino horn.

How many toes?

There are two groups of animals with hoofs. The odd-toed group is made up of the animals with one or three toes on each foot. These include horses, zebras and rhinos. Deer, camels, cows and sheep are some of the even-toed types. They have two or four toes on each foot.

Animals with hoofs eat plants. Their teeth are shaped to chew grass and leaves. Those that eat grass are called

▲ A mixed group of hoofed animals gather around an African waterhole. How many different types of animal can you see?

▼ The giraffe is the tallest animal in the world. Is it useful to be as tall as this?

grazers. They include sheep, cows and zebras. Some types eat the leaves of bushes or trees and they are called **browsers**. Most deer browse on small bushes. The giraffe is the tallest of all animals and can grow to six metres in height. Its long neck allows the giraffe to browse high up in the trees.

Living together

Many kinds of hoofed animal live in Africa. Sometimes several different types of animal mix together in one huge herd. They all find enough food because each type eats different plants. Some like the tender grasses. Others like long, coarse grasses. Other types of animal nibble at bushes. The tall giraffe eats tree leaves which are out of reach for all other animals.

All the animals help each other by staying in large herds. There are many pairs of eyes to watch out for enemies.

▼ This herd of wildebeeste is crossing an African river on its long journey to find more food.

Apes and monkeys

Apes, lemurs and monkeys belong to a group of mammals called the **primates**. We humans are also members of this large group. Most primates live in the trees. They have good eyesight to help them judge distances as they leap through the branches.

Monkeys and lemurs

Monkeys have long arms and tails, which help in moving through the trees. The long arms give them good reach. The long tails help them to keep their balance. Monkeys are divided into two main groups. One group, the New World monkeys, lives in South and Central America. Many New World monkeys have tails which can hold on to branches. They include spider monkeys, howler monkeys and marmosets. Most of them feed on leaves and fruit.

The other group, the Old World monkeys, lives in Africa and Asia. The Old World monkeys look slightly different from their New World cousins. They have narrower noses and do not have gripping tails. Some live in trees. They have very long legs, arms and tails. Baboons and macaques live on the ground, eating anything they can find.

Most monkeys live in large groups, or **troops**. This helps to protect them from enemies. Some troops contain family groups. Others are mixed and change size from day to day.

Lemurs and bush babies look like monkeys with long noses. These animals are active at night. They have large eyes to help them see in the dark. Lemurs live

chimpanz

gibbon

mandrill

gorilla

red howler
monkey

dwarf
lemur

barbary ape

only on the island of Madagascar. Bush babies live in tropical Africa. All live and feed in the trees.

Apes

The main difference between apes and monkeys is that apes have no tails. The apes are our closest animal relatives. They include the gorilla, chimpanzee and orang-utan. These types are known as the great apes. The gorilla and chimp are found in Africa. They stay mostly on the ground. The orang-utan lives in Borneo and Sumatra. It spends most of the time in the trees, moving slowly about in search of fruit.

The lesser apes, or gibbons, are a lot smaller than the great apes. Gibbons live in the forests of South East Asia. They are faster and noisier than the orang-utan. Their loud calls warn others off their territory. They also make noises to attract their mates.

Monkeys and apes come in different shapes and sizes.

diana monkey

The largest animals

There is something very splendid about elephants and whales. They are the largest animals. They need vast amounts of food each day to stay alive. Yet many of them live to be as old as humans. We do not want to see them dying out because of hunting.

In the sea

The blue whale is the largest animal ever to have lived. It is larger even than the dinosaurs. Blue whales have difficulty in finding enough food. Each day, a blue whale needs to eat two or more tonnes of small shrimps, called **krill**. They find the krill in swarms near the surface. As the seasons change, the whales follow the krill around the oceans.

Blue whales start to breed when they are about 20 years old. Then they produce young once every few years. At

▼ A humpback whale leaps right out of the water. Humpbacks live in both southern and northern oceans.

birth, the young whale is a large animal. It may be 7½m long. Whales do not produce young as often as most other animals.

Whales are killed for their meat, bones and oil. The largest whales are the most valuable. If too many of these are killed, the blue whale and other types could die out. The nations of the world are now trying to control whale hunting.

On land

The largest land animal alive today is the African elephant. A bull elephant can weigh seven tonnes or more and can be four metres tall. They are light on their feet, despite their weight. Their feet are wide and inside each foot there is a pad of spongy material. This helps to spread and cushion the animal's great weight.

▲ The African elephant is the biggest land mammal in the world. A fully-grown bull elephant can weigh as much as seven tonnes.

▼ A black rhino at full charge.

Elephants need a large amount of food. Each day, one animal eats about 150 kg of food and drinks up to 100 litres of water. They can eat many types of food. They even eat branches and the bark of trees.

Large land animals can be very fast movers. The rhinoceros can charge at a speed of 60 kph. When angry, an elephant can reach 40 kph. These animals can only run as fast as this over short distances.

Like all the large sea animals, the land giants have a long life. The Indian rhino can live for 45 years. Some elephants live for 80 years. Elephants and rhinos produce single young. A female may give birth only once in three years. If hunters were allowed to kill too many adults, then numbers would fall quickly. These large animals would soon die out.

Animals we must protect

We know that there are many different types of animal in the world. We, as humans, are just one type. We have large brains. We use these to think and plan.

Like many types of animal, we have always been hunters. In this, we are just the same as other predators, such as lions and tigers. We learned how to use spears and guns. Then we became the most deadly of all animals.

When guns were first made many people began to kill just for the sport. They killed elephants for their tusks. Tigers and other animals were killed for their skins. At one time there were many of these animals. Now some of them could become extinct.

Conservation

Throughout the world there are many groups of people who try to save wild animals. This is called **conservation**. The World Wildlife Fund is one of these groups. It is well known for its work to save the giant panda of China.

We also need to protect the places where some animals have chosen to live. In the world, there are many National Parks and Game Reserves. Here we can look at animals in their natural setting. These are places where rare animals have a chance to live and breed young.

▼ Many countries have stopped people hunting for sport, but animals are still killed by poachers. The World Wildlife Fund was set up to protect animals such as the giant panda.

Glossary

abdomen: the rear part of an insect's body, joined to the thorax

adult: a fully grown plant or animal

amphibian: an animal which starts life in water but lives on land when it is grown up. Frogs, toads and newts are amphibians

antenna: one of a pair of long feelers found on the heads of insects

antler: one of the pair of branched horns which grow from the heads of deer. They are shed each year

baleen: horny plates which grow inside the mouths of some types of whale. Baleen plates are used to catch the tiny animals which float in the sea

blowhole: a breathing hole, or nostril, in the top of the head of a whale

blubber: the thick layer of fat below the skin in sea mammals. Blubber stops body heat from escaping

browser: an animal which feeds on leaves, stems and twigs

cell: a very small part of a living thing. There are many different kinds of cell. Our bodies are made up of millions of cells

cold-blooded: describes animals that cannot control the temperature of their bodies. Their body temperature changes with the temperature of their surroundings

colony: a group of animals or plants that live together in the same area

conservation: the protection of animals and plants, and their natural surroundings

domestic: describes an animal that is tame and looked after by people

down: small, soft feathers of a bird. In adult birds, down feathers are found under the stiff, outer feathers. Young birds have only down feathers

evolve: to change slowly

exoskeleton: the hard outer covering of certain animals which gives them their shape

extinct: describes a type of animal which has died out completely

fossil: the hardened remains of an animal, or the shape of an animal, found in rock

gill: a part of the body which many water animals use for breathing. Not all water animals have gills

grazer: an animal which feeds on grass. Cows and sheep are grazing animals

hibernate: to spend the winter in a nesting or sleeping state

invertebrate: an animal which has no backbone. Worms, snails, insects and crabs are examples of invertebrates

krill: a small type of sea animal, like a shrimp

larva: a part of the life cycle of insects and other animals without backbones

lodge: a beaver's home

lung: a part of an animal used for breathing air

mammal: a warm-blooded animal which is usually covered with fur. Female mammals give birth to live young which feed on the mother's milk

mane: the long hair on the back of some animals' necks. Lions and horses have manes

marsupial: a mammal with a pouch. The young start life in the pouch

mimic: an animal imitator, or copy-cat. Some harmless insects mimic others that sting or bite

nestling: a young bird still in the nest

nymph: a stage in the life of some insects. Nymphs look like their parents, but do not have wings

plankton: tiny plants and animals that float near the surface of the sea and freshwater lakes. Plankton is a source of food for many water animals

predator: any animal that hunts and eats other animals

pride: a group of lions

primate: one of a group of mammals which includes monkeys, apes and humans

protozoa: one of a group of tiny animals with one cell

pupa: a stage in the life of some insects, such as butterflies and moths. A pupa does not eat or move

reptile: one of a group of cold-blooded animals with backbones and a dry, scaly skin. Snakes, lizards, crocodiles and turtles are reptiles

rodents: one of a group of small mammals with long front teeth which are used for gnawing

scale: one of the tiny flat 'plates' which cover the wings of butterflies and moths. Scales are made from a hair-like material

skeleton: the hard parts of an animal that support the rest of the body

soaring: rising high into the air without flapping the wings. To do this, birds are carried up by rising air currents

spawn: the eggs of frogs, toads and other amphibians

tadpole: a young stage in the life of frogs and toads. Tadpoles live in water and have tails and gills

teat: in mammals, a part of the body through which the young suck milk

territory: an area of land in which an animal or group of animals live, feed and breed. Animals mark out their territory by scent, or, in the case of birds, by singing

thorax: the middle part of an insect's body, between the head and the abdomen. The thorax supports the wings and legs

tide: the regular rise and fall of the surface of seas and oceans caused by the pull of the Sun and the Moon

troop: a group of monkeys

venom: a poison produced by snakes and other types of animal. Venom is injected into a body by a bite or sting

vertebrate: an animal with a backbone. Fish, amphibians, reptiles, birds and mammals are all vertebrates

warm-blooded: describes an animal whose body stays at the same temperature, whatever the temperature of its surroundings